Ketogenic Instant Pot Cookbook

100 Mouthwatering and Easy-to-Make Keto Delicacies for Your Power Pressure Cooker

By **Darlene V. Vanhoose**

Table of Contents

Introduction

Just because you have determined yourself to a life without carbs, doesn't mean that you should eat boring and tasteless meals.

If you think that Keto desserts are only strawberries and cream and Keto breakfasts only eggs and bacon, let this book show you that the meal combinations are pretty endless.

And if that doesn't make your life any easier, then perhaps this will. Introducing to you the revolutionary cooking appliance called *Instant Pot*, this cook book shows you the easiest, quickest, nutritious, and most delicious way to pressure cook your Keto meals.

From how to become (and stay) a Keto dieter to how to cook with the Instant Pot all while providing you with the ultimate cooking tips and 100 mouthwatering Instant Pot Keto delicacies, this book is the only cooking Keto guide you will ever need.

Now, throw away your apron, because this is the cleanest cooking you will ever see.

Join me on this yummy carbless ride and satisfy your cravings instantly.

The Ketogenic Guidelines

It seems that there is a low carb craze going on. More and more people decide to ditch the carbs and pack their bodies with fat. The low carb diets have surely extended their fan base largely this last decade, and the Ketogenic diet seems to be wearing the crown among them. But what exactly makes this diet so appealing and why should you embark the Keto train as well?

If you are a beginner who is willing to give this new 'trend' a go, you are probably concerned with a lot of things. *Will I faint if I stop eating carbs? Will I gain weight due to the increased fat intake? Will my cholesterol levels skyrocket?* These are just some of the many questions that people who are planning on starting the Keto diet ask themselves.

The answer? A firm "NO" to all of these questions. The Ketogenic diet will neither make you gain weight nor will it raise the LDL cholesterol levels. Quite the contrary. The ketogenic diet is a diet where you burn fat while eating fat.

The point of this diet is to shift your body fuel from carbs to ft. Because YES. Just like your body can run on carbs, it can run on fat just efficiently (if not even better!). By lowering the carb intake and increasing the fat, you will train your body to become dependent on the fat.

How Does it Work?

Once you lower the carb intake and stop consuming foods that are rich in fat, your body will be out of fuel. It will have an empty carb reservoir, so it will start looking elsewhere in order to energize itself and be able to continue working properly. Once it notices that there are no enough carbs left, the body will turn to fat to help. Then, it will start converting fat to energy, because it literally has no other option. Just think of a car that can run both on petrol and gas. When the petrol reservoir empties, the car will start using gas in order to get you from point A to point B. The same happens with the carb and fat fuel.

Just like your body converts the carbs into glucose, the same way it has to convert the fat in order to use it for energy. Fat gets converted into *ketones* (hence the name *KETOgenic*).

The whole point of this diet is to make your body use the ketones for energy. Once it starts doing that, you will reach a state of *ketosis*. The main goal of the Keto diet is to reach and stay in ketosis.

You will know that you have reached Ketosis if you start experiencing:

- Bad Breath
- Weight Loss
- Increased Focus
- Fatigue

I know that most of these symptoms aren't that appealing, but know that the process of 'getting used' to this diet lasts for about 2 weeks on average. It is a normal metabolic process that your body has to go through in order to become dependent on fat.

You can also measure your ketone levels in your blood or urine by buying special tests.

Is it Worth It?

Some people get so overwhelmed with the whole 'getting used to' process, that they decide to quit. If you are wondering whether 2 weeks of shaking off the carb addiction is worth it, maybe these benefits will make you make a decision. This is what the Ketogenic diet can provide you with and why it has become a growing trend:

- *Quick Weight Loss*
- *Loss in the Appetite* – once you reach Ketosis you will have decrease appetite for carbs or unhealthy foods
- *A Drop in the Blood Pressure*
- *A Drop in the Triglyceride Levels*
- *Balanced Blood Sugar*
- *Stress Relief*
- *Extended Lifespan*
- *Mental Clarity*

Know Your Macros

The Ketogenic Diet consist of the consumption of high fat, moderate protein, and low carb. However, keep in mind that you should track your daily intake, not every meal. For instance, if you decide to eat a meal that is high in protein and moderate in fat for lunch, that is totally acceptable. It is your overall daily intake of macro nutrients that it matters. As long you are consuming more fat, you are good to go.

These are the recommended Macros:

65 – 70% of Fat

25 – 30% of Protein

5 % of Carbohydrates

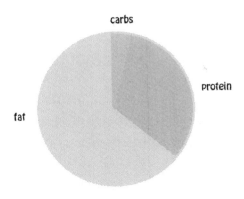

What to Eat?

Although being a Keto dieter surely involves more planning than simply eating whatever unhealthy food you are in the mood for, it is far from overwhelming.

There are many delicious ingredients that are allowed on the ketogenic diet (think dairy and bacon) that will help you prepare such finger-licking recipes that you will not even miss your junk food pleasures.

Here is what is recommended to eat on the Keto Diet:

- Meat
- Processed Meat (*bacon, sausages, salami, hot dogs*)
- Seafood
- Eggs
- Full-Fat Dairy (*milk, yogurt, cream, cheeses*)
- Avocados
- Non-Starchy Vegetables (*cabbage, broccoli, cauliflower, asparagus, eggplants, tomatoes, peppers, Brussel sprouts, onion, zucchini, leafy greens, squash, etc.*)
- Fruits (*consume in moderation because they are higher in carbs. Berries are the safest option*)
- Nuts
- Seeds
- Oils (*olive oil, avocado oil, coconut oil, flaxseed oil, macadamia oil*)

What <u>NOT</u> to Eat:

- Sugar
- Trans Fats
- Grains
- Diet Soda
- Fruit Juices
- Starchy Vegetables (*potatoes, beans, lentils, peas, corn, parsnips, etc.*)
- Refined Oils and Fats

The Keto Swaps

This wouldn't be an ultimate guide if it failed to explain to you how to exactly substitute for your carb cravings. There are a lot of Keto choices that can be used instead of the unhealthy carb-loaded ingredients that you may be in the mood of.

Here are the ultimate Keto swaps that will help you maintain the right course:

All-Purpose Flour → Almond Flour, Coconut Flour

Rice → Cauliflower Rice (ground in a food processor)

Baked Goods → You can eat muffins, bread, cakes, and cookies, as long as you substitute the sugar for a sweetener, and the flour for a nut flour. As long as it is low-carb, you can safely consume it.

Pasta and Spaghetti → Spiralized Vegetables such as Zoodles (zucchini noodles) or Spaghetti Squash

Mashed Potatoes → Mashed low-carb veggies such as Cauliflower

Bread Crumbs → Ground Nuts

Lasagna Noodles → Eggplant or Zucchini Slices

Potato Chips → Zucchini, kale, or apple chips

Cooking with Instant Pot

Whether you have already bought it or you are thinking about buying an instant pot, know that this revolutionary appliance will be the star of your kitchen and your new best friend. Why? Because it replaces 7 different kitchen gadgets. That being said, you can use your one and not-expensive Instant Pot for 7 different cooking methods:

1. A Pressure Cooker
2. A Saute Pan
3. A Slow Cooker
4. A Steamer
5. A Rice Cooker
6. A Yogurt Maker
7. A Warming Pot

The Benefits

But, being a 7-in-1 appliance is not the only benefit that the revolutionary Instant Pot provides with. There are a number of reasons why you should switch to pressure cooking with the instant pot:

It's Time Efficient-If you are a busy worker (and who isn't nowadays) then your time is most likely pretty limited. The instant pot can provide you with the chance to start home cooking again because it actually cooks the meals 70 percent faster than other appliances.

It Saves Money-The main benefit of the Instant Pot is the fact that it saves energy. Cooking 70 percent faster means using 70 percent less energy than other appliances, which cuts your electric bill significantly. Another way in which the Instant Pot can save you money is that it turns even the cheapest cuts of meats into restaurant-like incredible dishes.

Nutrient Preserving-Thanks to the pressure flow that circles inside the pot, the meals are cooked even, and all of the nutrients are preserved.

No Harmful Substances-Pressure cooking means cooking at a temperature that is higher than the point of boiling water. That being said, all of the harmful substances found on the food are lost during the process of cooking.

It is Convenient-Cooking has really never been easier. You ca simply dump your ingredients in the pot, close the lid, set the cooking mode and time, and you will get delicious results minutes later.

How can the IP Help on Your Keto Journey?

Instant Pot is great, there is no doubt about that, bit in which way can actually help you on your Ketogenic Journey?

Following such a restrictive diet such as the Ketogenic diet, a balance nutrient intake is quite important for your overall health. Starches are harmful, but some of the starchy foods contain extremely healthy properties. But since the Keto diet forbids them, you will need to get them elsewhere.

That said, it is important to get the most out of the ingredients that you are allowed to eat.

Unlike steaming food, where most of the vitamins and minerals are lost during the process of cooking, the Instant Pot preserves all of nutrients that can be found in the food. Cooking with the Instant Pot help you balance your diet and ensure that you are providing your body with all of the essential nutrients.

The Buttons

At the first glance, the Instant Pot may look quite overwhelming, thanks to the fact that there are quite a few button that can be found on the appliance. But the buttons aren't there to make Instant cooking daunting, but a simple and convenient experience.

Here is what each button mean:

Manual Button – The manual button is the standard cooking button. It is the most used button, and in fact, you ca cook all of your meals with this button if you choose to. It allows you to set your own cooking time, manually.

"+" and "-" – With the help of these buttons you can choose to increase or decrease the cooking time.

Adjust Button – This button will adjust the setting to the in-build mode that they have by default.

Pressure Button – With the help of this button you can switch from low to high pressure and vice versa.

Keep Warm/Cancel – By pressing this button you can either keep your meal warm until ready to open and serve, or you can cancel the cooking.

Slow Cook Button – With this, the Instant Pot works as a slow cooker.

Steam Button – The default is set for 10 minutes of cooking, and this button steams veggies and fish to perfection.

Yogurt Button – If you want to make yogurt or pasteurize milk, you can do that by pressing this button.

Rice Button – Great for cooking rice. This cooks automatically on LOW, but that can be changed.

Meat/Stew Button – If you want to cook meat or stew, a simple click on this button will cook on 35 minutes default. Change that if you want to cook longer than that.

Bean/Chili – Its default setting of 30 minutes will cook chilies and dished made with beans to perfection.

Poultry Button – If you have chicken or turkey to be cooked, a click on this button will cook for 15 minutes and to perfection.

Soup Button – This button is a convenient way to make soups. Its default setting is 30 minutes.

Porridge Button – Make porridges by pressing this button.

Multigrain Button – If you have grains to be cooked (although you are not concerned with this), you can cook them perfectly with this button.

What about the Pressure?

It may seem complicated to pressure cook your meals, but the Instant Pot is the most hassle-free appliance among its fellow pressure cookers. There are two ways in which you can release the pressure:

Naturally – When the food you are cooking is larger in volute, is foamy, or has a high liquid content, a natural pressure release is required in order to prevent leaking.

Quickly – If you choose this method, you will let the pressure out of the pot quickly and all at once. You can use this with seafood, veggies, or even meat. Just make sure that your pot isn't full because it will result in spillage.

Tips for Instant Cooking

Here are some simple tips that will make your cooking with the Instant Pot a convenient, safe, and wonderful experience:

- NEVER force open the lid. The pressure must be fully released before you decide to open the lid. This is the only way to prevent yourself from getting burned, or even other injuries.
- NEVER overfill the Instant Pot. If you put too much food inside and overcrowd the Instant Pot, that may clog the valve and in turn increase the cooking pressure. Never fill it more than 2/3 of the way. Pay attention if the food you are cooking can double in size. In that case, fill only halfway though.
- Too much liquid can dilute the flavor and taste. 1 ½ cups of liquid is the perfect rule of a thumb for Instant cooking.
- If the foods you are about to cook is frozen, increase the cooking times by a few minutes, depending on what you are cooking.
- Check the sealing rings regularly. The rule is to replace them after 18 months, but check them regularly to make sure that they are not deformed.

Breakfast Recipes

Herbed Eggs ✓++

(Total Time: 15 MIN| Serves: 4)

Ingredients:

- 7 Eggs
- ¼ - ½ cup Milk
- 4 ounces Bacon, diced
- 1 tsp Thyme
- ¼ cup chopped Fresh Parsley
- 2 tbsp chopped Cilantro
- ½ tsp Garlic Powder
- ¼ tsp Salt
- 1 ½ cups Water

Needs more spice

Directions:

1. Whisk together the eggs, milk, thyme, chopped herbs, salt, and garlic powder.
2. Set the Instant Pot to SAUTE and place the diced bacon in it.

16

3. Cook for 2 minutes, or until the bacon becomes crispy.
4. Transfer the bacon to a greased baking pan that can fit into your Instant Pot.
5. Pour the egg mixture over.
6. Pour the water into the IP and lower the trivet.
7. Place the baking dish inside and close the lid.
8. Set the IP to MANUAL and cook on HIGH for 20 minutes.
9. Release the pressure quickly.
10. Serve and enjoy!

(Calories 290 | Total Fats 24 g | Net Carbs: 4.5g | Protein 16g)

Breakfast Bagels

(Total Time: 30 MIN| Serves: 3)

Ingredients:

- ¾ cup Almond or Coconut Flour

- 1 ½ cups shredded Mozzarella Cheese
- 1/8 cup Cream Cheese
- 1 Egg
- 1 tsp Xanthan Gum
- 1 tbsp Butter, melted
- Pinch of Sea Salt
- 1 ½ cups Water

Directions:

1. Pour the water into the Instant Pot and lower the rack.
2. Whisk together the eggs, salt, and xanthan gum.
3. Place the mozzarella in a microwave-safe bowl and microwave until melted.
4. Add the melted cheese to the egg mixture along with the flour.
5. Mix until a ball of dough is formed.
6. Divide the dough into 3 equal pieces.
7. Make three bagels out of the dough and flatten them with your hand.
8. Grease a baking dish with cooking spray and place the bagels on it.
9. Brush the melted butter over them.
10. Place in the IP and close the lid.
11. Choose MANUAL and cook for 15 minutes.
12. Do a quick pressure release.
13. Cut the bagels in half and serve with your favorite toppings.Enjoy!

(Calories 370| Total Fats 30g | Net Carbs: 3.5g | Protein 20g)

Chia and Coconut Breakfast Puddung

(Total Time: 10 MIN| Serves: 4)

Ingredients:

- ½ cup Chia Seeds
- ¼ cup chopped Almonds
- 2 cups Almond Milk
- 4 tsp Sweetener
- ¼ cup shredded Coconut

Directions:

1. Place everything in the Instant Pot.
2. Stir to combine the ingredients well.
3. Close the lid and choose the MANUAL cooking mode.
4. Cook on HIGH for 3 minutes.
5. Release the pressure quickly.
6. Divide the pudding between 4 serving bowls or glasses.Enjoy!

(Calories 130| Total Fats 12g | Net Carbs: 1.5g | Protein 14g)

Cheesy Cauliflower Egg Pie

(Total Time: 30 MIN| Serves: 6)

Ingredients:

- 8 Eggs, whisked
- ½ Onion, diced
- 1 tsp Garlic Salt
- 1 tsp dried Thyme
- 8 ounces grated Mozzarella Cheese
- 2 ounces grated Cheddar Cheese
- ¼ tsp Turmeric
- 2 cups Cauliflower Rice (ground in a food processor)
- ¼ tsp Pepper
- 1 ½ cups Water

Directions:

1. Pour the water into the Instant Pot and lower the trivet.
2. Place everything in a large bowl and stir to combine.

3. Grease a pie pan with some cooking spray.
4. Pour the cheesy cauliflower mixture into it.
5. Place the pan in the Instant Pot and close the lid.
6. Cook on HIGH for 20 minutes.
7. Press CANCEL and wait 5 minutes before doing a quick pressure release.
8. Serve and enjoy!

(Calories 350| Total Fats 25g | Net Carbs: 5.2g | Protein 17g)

Cinnamon Cream Cheese Pancakes

(Total Time: 15 MIN| Serves: 2)

Ingredients:

- 4 Eggs
- 4 ounces Cream Cheese
- 1 ½ tbsp Butter
- 2 tsp Sweetener
- 1 tsp Cinnamon

Directions:

1. Set your Instant Pot to SAUTE and melt some of the butter in it.
2. Meanwhile, whisk tougher the eggs, cinnamon, sweetener, and cream cheese.
3. Add some of the batter to the IP and cook for 2-3 minutes.
4. Flip over and cook for additional minute.
5. Repeat with the other pancakes.
6. Serve with your favorite toppings and enjoy!

(Calories 340| Total Fats 29g | Net Carbs: 3g | Protein 17g)

Feta and Olive Omelet

(Total Time: 30 MIN| Serves: 2)

Ingredients:

- 6 Eggs
- 2 tbsp Milk

- ¼ tsp Pepper
- ½ tsp Garlic Salt
- A handful of diced Olives
- ¼ cup Feta Cheese, cubed
- A handful of Olive Slices
- 1 ½ cups Water

Directions:

1. Pour the water into the Instant Pot and lower the rack.
2. Whisk together the eggs, milk, salt, and pepper.
3. Stir in the diced olives.
4. Grease a baking dish with some cooking spray and pour the egg mixture into it.
5. Place the dish in the IP and close the lid.
6. Cook on HIGH for 15-20 minutes, depending on the desired consistency.
7. Do a quick pressure release.
8. Top the cooked eggs with feta cubes and olives
9. Serve and enjoy!

(Calories 300| Total Fats 15g | Net Carbs: 3g | Protein 14g)

Sausage-Wrapped Eggs

(Total Time: 20 MIN| Serves: 4)

Ingredients:

- 1 pound ground Sausage
- 4 Hardboiled Eggs
- 1 cup Water
- 1 tbsp Olive Oil

Directions:

1. Peel the eggs and divide the sausage into 4 equal pieces.
2. Flatten each piece of sausage and place an egg on top.
3. Wrap the sausage around the egg completely. Repeat with the remaining eggs and sausage.
4. Heat the oil in the IP on SAUTE and add the eggs.
5. Cook for 2 minutes or until the sausage is slightly browned.
6. Transfer to a plate.
7. Pour the water into the Instant Pot and lower the rack.

8. Arrange the eggs on the rack and close the lid.
9. Cook for 6 minutes on HIGH.
10. Release the pressure quickly.
11. Serve and enjoy!

(Calories 615| Total Fats 50g | Net Carbs: 2.5g | Protein 33g)

Sausage Shakshuka ✓+++

(Total Time: 30 MIN| Serves: 3)

Ingredients:

- ¾ pound Ground Sausage
- 4 Eggs
- 1/3 cup diced Onion
- 1 tbsp Coconut Oil
- ¼ tsp Pepper
- 1 tsp Cumin
- 1 Red Bell Pepper, diced
- 24 ounces diced Tomatoes
- 1 tsp Garlic Powder
- ½ tsp Salt
- 1 ½ cups Water

Directions:

1. Melt the coconut oil in the IP on SAUTE.
2. Add the bell pepper and onion and cook for 3 minutes, until soft.
3. Stir in cumin and garlic powder and cook for another minute.
4. Add the sausage and cook, while breaking it up, for a few minutes.
5. Stir in the tomatoes and transfer the mixture to a greased baking dish.
6. Crack the eggs on top.
7. Pour the water into the Instant Pot and lower the rack.
8. Place the dish in the IP and close the lid.
9. Cook on HIGH for 10 minutes.
10. Serve and enjoy!

(Calories 502| Total Fats 38g | Net Carbs: 7g | Protein 28g)

Zucchini Breakfast Bread with Walnuts

(Total Time: 50 MIN| Serves: 16)

Ingredients:

- 2 ½ cups Almond or Coconut Flour
- 3 Eggs
- 1 ½ tsp Baking Powder
- ½ cup Olive Oil
- ½ cup chopped or ground Walnuts
- ½ tsp Vanilla
- ¼ tsp Nutmeg
- 1 cup grated Zucchini
- Pinch of Sea Salt
- 1 ½ cups Water

Directions:

1. Pour the water into your Instant Pot and lower the trivet.
2. Combine the dry ingredients in a bowl.

3. Whisk together all of the wet ingredients in another bowl.
4. Combine the two mixtures together.
5. Stir in the zucchini and walnuts.
6. Transfer to a greased loaf pan and place in the IP.
7. Close the lid and choose MANUAL.
8. Cook on HIGH for 35 minutes.
9. Serve and enjoy!

(Calories | Total Fats 29g | Net Carbs: 3.5g | Protein 20g)

Creamy Eggs with Chives

(Total Time: 15 MIN| Serves: 4)

Ingredients:

- 4 tbsp Heavy Cream
- 4 Eggs
- 1 ½ tbsp chopped Chives
- Pinch of Salt
- Pinch of Pepper
- 1 ½ cups Water

Directions:

1. Pour the water into your IP and lower the trivet.
2. Coat 4 ramekins with some cooking spray.
3. Add a tablespoon of heavy cream to each ramekin.
4. Crack the eggs into the ramekins.
5. Season with salt and pepper.
6. Top with chopped chives.
7. Place the ramekin in the IP and close the lid.
8. Cook on MANUAL for 2 minutes.
9. Release the pressure quickly.
10. Serve and enjoy!

(Calories 170| Total Fats 17g | Net Carbs: 0.9g | Protein 6g)

Jalapeno and Cheddar Eggs

(Total Time: 25 MIN| Serves: 6)

Ingredients:

- 12 Eggs
- 4 Jalapeno Peppers, chopped
- ¼ tap Garlic Salt
- ¼ tsp Pepper
- Pinch of Cumin
- 1 cup shredded Cheddar Cheese
- 1 ½ cups Water

Directions:

1. Pour the water into the Instant Pot. Lower the triver.
2. Whisk together the eggs and spices.
3. Stir in the chopped jalapenos and cheddar.
4. Divide between 6 jars.
5. Seal the jars and place inside the Instant Pot.
6. Choose MANUAL and cook on HIGH for 8 minutes.
7. Let the pressure release naturally, about 10 minutes.
8. Serve and enjoy!

(Calories 220| Total Fats 16g | Net Carbs: 2g | Protein 18g)

Cheesy Tomato and Spinach Egg Cups

(Total Time: 10 MIN| Serves: 4

Ingredients:

- ¼ cup crumbled Feta Cheese
- 6 Eggs
- 1 cup chopped Spinach
- 1 Tomato, diced
- ½ cup shredded Mozzarella Cheese
- ¼ tsp Garlic Powder
- Salt and Pepper, to taste

Directions:

1. Pour the water into the Instant Pot. Lower the trivet.
2. Whisk the eggs and spices together.
3. Add the tomato, feta, and mozzarella, and stir to combine.
4. Grease 4 ramekins with cooking spray.
5. Divide the spinach between the ramekins.
6. Pour the cheesy egg mixture over.
7. Arrange the ramekins inside the IP and close the lid.
8. Cook on HIGH for 8 minutes.
9. Serve and enjoy!

(Calories 115| Total Fats 7g | Net Carbs: 2g | Protein 10.5g)

Soups and Stews

Tomato and Basil Soup

(Total Time: 30 MIN| Serves: 4)

Ingredients:

- ½ Onion, diced
- 28 ounces canned Tomatoes
- 2 tbsp Tomato Paste
- A handful of Basil, chopped
- 1 tbsp Olive Oil
- 3 cups Veggie Broth
- 1 tsp Balsamic Vinegar

Directions:

1. Heat the oil in your IP on SAUTE.
2. Add onions and cook for 3 minutes.
3. Stir in the tomato paste and cook for one more minute.
4. Add tomatoes and broth.
5. Close the lid and choose the SOUP mode.
6. Cook for 10 minutes.

7. Let the pressure release naturally.
8. Stir in the vinegar and half of the basil.
9. Blend the soup with a hand blender.
10. Top with the remaining basil.
11. Serve and enjoy!

(Calories 100| Total Fats 4.5g | Net Carbs: 9.2g | Protein 2g)

Chicken and Spinach Soup

(Total Time: 40 MIN| Serves: 4)

Ingredients:

- 1 pound Chicken, chopped
- 1 tsp Garlic Powder
- ½ Onion, diced
- 1 cup Spinach
- ½ Fennel Bulb, chopped
- 2 cups Chicken Broth
- 4 Green Onions, chopped
- Sal and Pepper, to taste

Directions:

1. Place everything in your Instant Pot.
2. Stir to combine the ingredients well.
3. Close the lid and choose the SOUP cooking mode.
4. Cook for 30 minutes.

5. Release the pressure naturally.
6. Serve and enjoy!

(Calories 180| Total Fats 2.2g | Net Carbs: 4g | Protein 24g)

Creamy Asparagus Soup

(Total Time: 15 MIN| Serves: 4)

Ingredients:

- ¼ Onion, diced
- 5 cups Bone Broth
- 1 ½ pounds Asparagus, trimmed and chopped
- 8 ounces Sour Cream
- 3 tbsp Butter
- 1 tsp Salt
- ¼ tsp Pepper
- ½ tsp minced Garlic

Directions:

1. Melt the butter in your IP on SAUTE.
2. Add the onions and cook for 2 minutes.
3. Add garlic and cook for 30 more seconds.

4. Stir in the remaining ingredients.
5. Close the lid and set your IP to MANUAL.
6. Cook on HIGH for 5 minutes.
7. Release the pressure naturally.
8. Serve and enjoy!

(Calories 300| Total Fats 6g | Net Carbs: 7g | Protein 8)

No Bean Chili

(Total Time: 45 MIN| Serves: 4)

Ingredients:

- 1 pound ground Beef
- 1 tsp Garlic Powder
- 1 tbsp Olive Oil
- 1 ½ cups Beef Broth
- 28 ounces canned Tomatoes
- ½ tbsp Cumin
- 2 tbsp Tomato Paste
- 1 ½ tbsp Chili Powder
- ½ Onion, diced

Directions:

1. Heat the oil in your Instant Pot on SAUTE.
2. Add the onions and cook for 3 minutes.
3. Add beef and cook until it becomes browned.
4. Stir in the spices and tomato paste, and cook for one more minute.
5. Add the remaining ingredients, stir, and close the lid.
6. Cook on SOUP for 30 minutes.
7. Serve and enjoy!

(Calories 380| Total Fats 28g | Net Carbs: 9g | Protein 21g)

Quick Tofu and Miso Soup

(Total Time: 12 MIN| Serves: 4)

Ingredients:

- ½ Onion, diced
- 1 cup cubed Silken Tofu
- 4 cups Water
- 2 tbsp Miso Paste
- ½ cup Celery cubes
- 1 Carrot, chopped
- 1 tbsp Tamari Sauce
- 2 Celery Stalks, chopped

Directions:

1. Place all of the ingredients, except the miso, in your Instant Pot.
2. Close the lid and choose the POULTRY cooking mode.
3. Cook for 7 minutes.
4. Do a quick pressure release.
5. Take some of the soup and whisk the miso paste in it.
6. Stir the mixture into the soup.
7. Serve and enjoy!

(Calories 80| Total Fats 3g | Net Carbs: 2.5g | Protein 3.5g)

Kale and Sausage Soup

(Total Time: 25 MIN| Serves: 6)

Ingredients:

- 1 pound Sausage, sliced
- 4 Bacon Slices, diced
- 2 cups chopped Kale
- ¼ cup Water
- 1 cup Heavy Cream
- 1 ½ quarts Chicken Broth
- ½ Onion, diced
- 1 tsp minced Garlic
- 1 cup low-carb Veggies by choice, chopped
- Salt and Pepper, to taste

Directions:

1. Set the Instant Pot to SAUTE.
2. Add bacon and cook until crispy.
3. Transfer the cooked bacon to a plate and add the onions to the Instant Pot.
4. Saute for 3 minutes.
5. Add the garlic and cook for 1 more minute
6. Add the sausage slices and cook until browned.
7. Stir in the remaining ingredients and close the lid.
8. Cook on HIGH for 3 minutes.
9. Release the pressure naturally, for about 10 minutes.
10. Season with some salt and pepper before serving.
11. Serve and enjoy!

(Calories 320| Total Fats 35g | Net Carbs: 8g | Protein 28g)

Simple Beef Stew

(Total Time: 40 MIN| Serves: 4)

Ingredients:

- 1 pound Beef, chopped into cubes
- 28 ounces diced canned Tomatoes, undrained
- 3 cups Beef Broth
- 1 Carrot, sliced
- ½ Onion, diced
- 2 tsp minced Garlic
- 1 Red Bell Pepper, diced
- 1 Bay Leaf
- 1 tsp Thyme
- 1 tbsp Olive Oil
- 2 tbsp chopped Parsley

Directions:

1. Heat the oil in your Instant Pot on SAUTE.
2. Saute the onions and peppers for 3 minutes.
3. Add garlic and thyme and cook for one more.
4. Add the beef and cook until browned.
5. Stir in the remaining ingredients.
6. Close the lid and choose the MANUAL cooking mode.
7. Cook on HIGH for 20 minutes.
8. Wait 5 minutes before doing a quick pressure release.
9. Serve and enjoy!

(Calories 363| Total Fats 32g | Net Carbs: 6g | Protein 30g)

Turkey and Broccoli Stew

(Total Time: 30 MIN| Serves: 4)

Ingredients:

- 1 cup Broccoli Florets
- 2 Celery Stalks, chopped
- 1 tsp Thyme
- 2 tbsp Ghee or Butter
- 1 Carrot, sliced
- ½ Onion, diced
- 3 ½ cups Chicken Broth
- 1 pound Turkey Breast, cubed
- ½ tsp Garlic Powder

Directions:

1. Melt the ghee in your IP on SAUTE.
2. Add the onions and saute for 3 minutes.
3. Stir in garlic and thyme and cook for an additional minute.
4. Add carrots and celery and cook for 2 minutes.
5. Place the turkey cubes inside and cook until no longer pink.
6. Stir in the remaining ingredients and close the lid.
7. Choose MANUAL and cook on HIGH for 6 minutes.
8. Let the pressure drop naturally, about 10-15 minutes.
9. Serve and enjoy!

(Calories 240| Total Fats 15g | Net Carbs: 4.9g | Protein 25g)

Two-Meat Soup

(Total Time: 45 MIN| Serves: 4)

Ingredients:

- ½ Onion, diced
- 3 cups Bone Broth
- 1 cup cooked and shredded Chicken Meat
- ¼ Cabbage, sliced
- 4 Ounces Spinach, chopped
- ½ cup cohpped Celery
- ½ tsp Turmeric
- 1 tsp Thyme
- ¼ Cauliflower Rice

Meatballs:

- ½ pound ground Beef
- ½ tsp Oregano
- ½ tsp Garlic Powder

Directions:

1. Combine the meatball ingredients and shape into small meatballs.
2. Place in the Instant Pot.Pour the broth over.
3. Stir in the remaining ingredients, except the chicken.
4. Close the lid and set your Instant Pot to SOUP.
5. Cook for 30 minutes.
6. Do a quick pressure release and stir in the chicken.
7. Serve and enjoy!

(Calories 260| Total Fats 15g | Net Carbs: 4.9g | Protein 20g)

Cheesy Broccoli Soup

(Total Time: 30 MIN| Serves: 6)

Ingredients:

- 1 cup Pepper Jack Cheese, grated
- 4 American Cheese Slices, chopped
- 3 cups Veggie Broth41 tsp paprika
- 2 tbsp Almond Flour
- 2 tbsp Butter
- 2 Carrots, chopped
- 5 cups Broccoli Florets
- 1 tsp Dill
- 1 tsp minced Garlic
- 1 cup Colby Jack Cheese, shredded
- ½ cup grated Parmesan Cheese
- 1 cup Half and Half

Directions:

1. Melt the butter in your Instant Pot and add the carrots and onion.
2. Cook for 3 minutes until soft.

3. Add garlic and flour and cook for one more minute.
4. Add the broth and broccoli, and stir to combine.
5. Close the lid and cook on HIGH for 8 minutes.
6. Press CANCEL and do a quick pressure release.
7. Stir the remaining ingredients.
8. Blend with a hand blender until smooth.
9. Serve immediately.
10. Enjoy!

(Calories 320| Total Fats 17g | Net Carbs: 6g | Protein 8g)

Fish Stew

(Total Time: 20 MIN| Serves: 6)

Ingredients:
- 1 Onion, diced
- 1 Carrot, sliced
- 2 Celery Stalks, chopped
- 1 1/2 cup Cauliflower Rice
- 1 cup chopped Broccoli
- 1 pound White Fish Fillets, chopped
- 1 Bay Leaf
- 1 cup Heavy Cream
- 3 cups Fish Broth
- 2 tbsp Butter
- ½ tsp Salt

- ¼ tsp Pepper
- ¼ tsp Garlic Powder

Directions:

1. Melt the butter in your Instant Pot on SAUTE.
2. Add carrots and onions and cook for 3 minutes.
3. Add the remaining ingredients and stir to combine well.
4. Close the lid and choose the MANUAL cooking mode.
5. Cook on HIGH for 4 minutes.
6. Let the pressure come down naturally.
7. Remove the bay leaf before serving.
8. Serve and enjoy

(Calories 165| Total Fats 17g | Net Carbs: 4.5g | Protein 22g)

Mexican Chicken Soup

(Total Time: 15 MIN| Serves: 8)

Ingredients:

- 2 cups cooked and shredded Chicken
- 8 cups Chicken Broth
- 1 tbsp Cumin
- ½ tsp minced Habanero
- 1 cup Celery, cubed
- ½ cup chopped Cilantro
- 4 ounces canned Chilies, chopped
- ½ cup chopped Scallions
- 1/3 cup Salsa
- 1 tsp Garlic Powder
- 1 tsp Onion Powder

Directions:

1. Place everything in your Instant Pot.
2. Stir to combine the mixture well.
3. Close the lid and set the IP to SAUTE.
4. Cook the soup for 10 minutes.
5. Press CANCEL and let the pressure release quickly.
6. Serve and enjoy!

(Calories 100| Total Fats 5g | Net Carbs: 3g | Protein 11g)

Appetizers, Sides, and Snacks

Mashed Cauliflower

(Total Time: 12 MIN| Serves: 4)

Ingredients:

- 1 large Cauliflower Head, chopped
- 1 cup Water
- 1 tbsp Butter
- Pinch of Pepper
- ½ tsp Salt

Directions:

1. Pour the water into the Instant Pot and lower the steaming basket
2. Place the cauliflower in the steaming basket and close the lid.
3. Set your Instant Pot to MANUAL.
4. Cook on HIGH for 3-5 minutes.
5. Release the pressure quickly.

6. Mash the cauliflower with a potato masher and stir in the remaining ingredients.
7. Serve and enjoy!

(Calories 180| Total Fats 6g | Net Carbs: 2g | Protein 3g)

Sesame Bok Choy

(Total Time: 10 MIN| Serves: 4)

Ingredients:

- 1 Bok Choy
- 1 tsp Soy Sauce
- ½ tsp Sesame Oil
- 2 tsp Sesame Seeds
- Pinch of Garlic Salt
- 1 ½ cups Water

Directions:

1. Pour the water into your Instant Pot and lower the basket.
2. Place the bok choy in the steaming basket and close the lid.
3. Set the IP to MANUAL and cook on HIGH for 4 minutes.
4. Do a quick pressure release.
5. Chop the bok choy and place in a bowl.
6. Add the remaining ingredients.
7. Toss to combine well.

8. Serve and enjoy!

(Calories 55| Total Fats 3g | Net Carbs: 4g | Protein 2g)

Zesty and Citrusy Broccoli and Cauliflower Bowl

(Total Time: 20 MIN| Serves: 4)

Ingredients:

- 1 Cauliflower Head, broken into florets
- 1 pound Broccoli Florets
- 2 Oranges, sliced
- Juice and Zest from 1 Orange
- 1 tbsp Capers
- ½ tsp Salt
- ¼ tsp Pepper
- 4 tbsp Olive Oil
- 1 ½ cups Water

Directions:

1. Pour the water into your Instant Pot and lower the steaming basket.
2. Place the broccoli and cauliflower in it and close the lid.
3. Set your Instant Pot to STEAM.
4. Cook for 6 minutes.

5. While the veggies are cooking, whisk together the juice, zest, pepper, salt, oil, and capers, in a small bowl.
6. Release the pressure quickly.
7. Transfer the broccoli and cauliflower to a bowl and drizzle the dressing over.
8. Garnish with orange slices.
9. Serve and enjoy!

(Calories 240| Total Fats 8g | Net Carbs: 10g | Protein 3g)

Beets and Cheese

(Total Time: 35 MIN| Serves: 6)

Ingredients:

- 6 Beets, trimmed
- ¼ tsp Pepper
- ½ tsp Salt
- ¼ cup crumbled Cheese by choice

- 1 tbsp chopped Herbs
- 1 tbsp Olive Oil
- 1 ½ cups Water

Directions:

1. Pour the water into the Instant Pot and lower the rack.
2. Place the trimmed beets on the rack.
3. Close the lid and set the IP to MANUAL.
4. Cook on HIGH for 20 minutes.
5. Release the pressure quickly and let the beets cool until safe to handle.
6. Peel and chop the beets and transfer to a bowl.
7. Drizzle with olive oil and sprinkle with the herbs.
8. Season with salt and pepper.
9. Top with the crumbled cheese.
10. Serve and enjoy!

(Calories 70 | Total Fats 3g | Net Carbs: 8g | Protein 2.5g)

Bacon-Wrapped Asparagus

(Total Time: 15 MIN| Serves: 4)

Ingredients:

- 1 pound of Asparagus
- 8 ounces of Bacon, sliced
- 1 ½ cup of Water

Directions:

1. Pour the water into the Instant Pot. Lower the steaming basket.
2. Trim the asparagus and place inside the steaming bsket.
3. Close the lid and set the Instant Pot to Poultry.
4. Cook for 4 minutes.
5. Release the pressure quickly.
6. Wrap the bacon around the asparagus.
7. Discard the water from the IP and set it to SAUTE.
8. Place the wrapped asparagus and cook until the bacon becomes crispy.
9. Serve and enjoy!

(Calories 225| Total Fats 15g | Net Carbs: 5.7g | Protein 15g)

Garlicky Kale Chips

(Total Time: 15 MIN| Serves: 4)

Ingredients:

- 1 pound Kale
- 1 tbsp Olive Oil
- 2 tsp minced Garlic
- 2 tbsp Lemon Juice

Directions:

1. Heat the oil in your Instant Pot on SAUTE.
2. Add the garlic and cook for 1 minute, until fragrant.
3. Add the kale and cook until it becomes crispy.
4. Serve drizzled with lemon juice.
5. Enjoy!

(Calories 66| Total Fats 4g | Net Carbs: 5g | Protein 2g)

Devilled Eggs

(Total Time: 20 MIN| Serves: 4)

Ingredients:

- 4 Eggs
- 1 tsp Dijon Mustard
- 1 tsp Paprika
- 1 tbsp Mayonnaise
- 1 cup of Water

Directions:

1. Combine the water and eggs in your Instant Pot.
2. Close the lid and set it to MANUAL.
3. Cook on HIGH for 5 minutes.
4. Release the pressure naturally.
5. Prepare and ice bath and place the eggs to chill.
6. When safe to handle, peel them.
7. Cut the eggs in half and scoop out the yolks.
8. Place the yolks in a bowl, along with the mayonnaise and mustard.
9. Fill the eggs with this mixture.
10. Sprinkle the eggs with paprika.
11. Serve and enjoy!

(Calories 100| Total Fats 8g | Net Carbs: 0.5g | Protein 6.5g)

Cauliflower Fritters

(Total Time: 25 MIN| Serves: 12)

Ingredients:
- 1 cup shredded Cheddar Cheese

- 1 cup ground Almonds
- 1 Cauliflower Head, chopped
- 3 tbsp Olive Oil
- 1 tsp Italian Seasoning
- ¼ cup grated Parmesan Cheese
- 2 Eggs
- Pinch of Pepper
- ½ tsp Salt
- ¼ tsp Garlic Powder
- 1 ½ cups Water

Directions:

1. Place the cauliflower in the microwave and microwave for 5 minutes.
2. Drain and place in a food processor. Pulse until ground.
3. Transfer the cauliflower to a bowl along with the remaining ingredients, except the oil, water and ¼ cheddar.
4. Mix with your hands until fully incorporated.
5. Make 12 patties out of the mixture.
6. Heat 1 tbsp oil in your IP on SAUTE.
7. Add 4 patties and cook until golden on all sides.
8. Repeat this two more times.
9. Pour the water in your IP and lower the rack.
10. Place the fritters in a greased baking dish and in the IP.
11. Cook for 3 minutes on MANUAL.

12. Release the pressure quickly.
13. Top with the remaining cheese.
14. Serve and enjoy!

(Calories 120| Total Fats 7g | Net Carbs: 2.7g | Protein 2.8g)

Instant Garlicky Asparagus

(Total Time: 10 MIN| Serves: 4)

Ingredients:

- 1 pound Asparagus Spears, trimmed
- 1 tbsp diced Onion
- ¼ tsp Garlic Powder
- 2 tsp minced Garlic
- 2 tbsp Olive Oil
- 1 ½ cups Water

Directions:

1. Pour the water into the Instant Pot. Lower the trivet.
2. Arrange the asparagus inside and drizzle with the olive oil, onion and garlic.
3. Close the lid and set the IP to STEAM.
4. Cook the asparagus for 2 minutes.
5. Do a quick pressure release.
6. Sprinkle with garlic powder and serve.
7. Enjoy!

(Calories 85| Total Fats 7g | Net Carbs: 4.5g | Protein 2.5g)

Candied Pecans

(Total Time: 30 MIN| Serves: 4)

Ingredients:

- 2 cups Pecan Halves
- Liquid Sweetener, to taste
- ½ tsp Cinnamon
- ½ cup plus 1 tbsp Water

Directions:

1. Place the pecans, sweetener, 1 tbsp water, and cinnamon, in your Instant Pot.
2. Set it t SAUTE and cook for 5 minutes.
3. Transfer to a lined baking dish.
4. Pour the remaining water into the Instant pot and lower the trivet.
5. Place the dish inside and close the lid.

6. Cook on HIGH for 12 pressure.
7. Serve and enjoy!

(Calories 250| Total Fats 38g | Net Carbs: 5g | Protein 5g)

Spicy and Nutty Kale

(Total Time: 10 MIN| Serves: 4)

Ingredients:

- 10 ounces Kale
- 1 cup Almonds
- ¼ cup Cashews
- 1 ½ cups Water
- 1 tbsp Favorite Seasoning
- 1 tbsp Parmesan Cheese
- 2 tsp Vinegar

Directions:

1. Pour the water in your Instant Pot and place the kale in the steaming basket.
2. Lower the basket and close the lid.
3. Set the Instant Pot on MANUAL and cook on HIGH for 4 minutes.
4. Meanwhile place the nuts and parmesan in a food processor. Pulse until ground.
5. Transfer the kale to a bowl and toss with the nuts.

6. Sprinkle with your favorite seasoning and drizzle the vinegar over. Enjoy!

(Calories 210| Total Fats 17g | Net Carbs: 9g | Protein 10g)

Lemony and Mustardy Artichokes

(Total Time: 40 MIN| Serves: 8)

Ingredients:

- 2 Artichokes
- Juice of 1 Lemon
- ¼ tsp Garlic Powder
- 1 Lemon Wedge
- ¼ tsp Salt
- Pinch of Pepper
- 1 ½ cups Water

Directions:

1. Pour the water in your Instant Pot and lower the steaming basket.

2. Wash the artichokes and trim them.
3. Rub them with the lemon wedge and place in the steaming basket.
4. Close the lid and set the IP to MANUAL.
5. Cook on HIGH for 20 minutes.
6. Let the pressure release on its own, about 10 minutes.
7. Season the artichokes with the spices and drizzle the lemon juice over.
8. Serve and enjoy!

(Calories 50| Total Fats 1g | Net Carbs: 6.5 | Protein 2g)

Poultry Recipes

Juicy Whole Chicken

(Total Time: 50 MIN| Serves: 10)

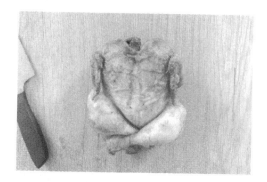

Ingredients:

- 1 tbsp Coconut Oil
- 1 ½ cups Chicken Stock
- 2 tbsp Lemon Juice
- 2 Garlic Cloves
- 3-4 pound Whole Chicken
- ½ tsp Salt
- ¼ tsp Black Pepper
- 1 tsp Onion Powder

Directions:

1. Season the chicken with salt, pepper, and onion powder.
2. Melt the coconut oil on SAUTE.
3. Place the chicken in side and cook on all sides, until golden brown.

4. Pour the stock and the lemon juice inside and add the garlic cloves.
5. Close the lid and set your IP to MANUAL.
6. Cook on HIGH for 25 minutes.
7. Release the pressure naturally.
8. Serve and enjoy!

(Calories 270| Total Fats 20g | Net Carbs: 3g | Protein 22g)

Hot Taco-Seasoned Chicken

(Total Time: 35 MIN| Serves: 6)

Ingredients:
- 1 ounce Taco Seasoning
- ½ cup Red Salsa
- ½ cup mild Salsa Verde
- 1 ½ pounds Chicken Breasts, skinless and boneless

Directions:
1. Place everything in the Instant Pot.
2. Stir to combine well and close the lid.
3. Set the Instant Pot to MANUAL.
4. Cook on HIGH for 25 minutes.
NO → 5. Do a quick pressure release. N PR
6. With two forks, shred the meat inside the pot.
7. Stir to combine and serve.

(Calories 240| Total Fats 9g | Net Carbs: 4.9g | Protein 33g)

Turkey Salsa Verde

(Total Time: 30 MIN| Serves: 6)

Ingredients:

- 2 ½ pounds Turkey Breasts, chopped into cubes
- 16 ounces Salsa Verde
- ¼ tsp Smoked Paprika
- ¼ tsp Garlic Salt
- ¼ tsp Black Pepper
- Pinch of Turmeric
- ¼ tsp Cumin

Directions:

1. Pour the salsa into your Instant Pot and add the spices.
2. Stir to combine well.
3. Place the turkey cubes inside and stir to coat well.
4. Close the lid and set the Instant Pot to MANUAL.
5. Cook on HIGH for 25 minutes.
6. Release the pressure quickly.
7. Serve and enjoy!

(Calories 340| Total Fats 7g | Net Carbs: 5g | Protein 40g)

Sweet Soy Sauce Drumsticks

(Total Time: 40 MIN| Serves: 5)

Ingredients:

- 10 smallish Chicken Drumsticks
- ½ cup Water
- ½ cup Soy Sauce
- 2 tsp Sweetener
- ¼ tsp Black Pepper
- ½ tsp Salt
- ½ tsp Garlic Powder
- 1 tsp dried Thyme

Directions:

1. Combine all of the spices in a small bowl.
2. Season the drumsticks by rubbing the mixture into the meat.
3. Whisk the soy sauce and water in your IP.
4. Place the drumsticks inside and close the lid.
5. Set the IP to MANUAL and cook for 25 minutes.
6. Do a quick pressure release.

7. Serve and enjoy!

(Calories 210| Total Fats 15.5g | Net Carbs: 3g | Protein 31.3g)

Barbecue Wings

(Total Time: 15 MIN| Serves: 2)

Ingredients:

- 12 Chicken Wings
- ¼ cup Barbecue Sauce, sugar-free
- 1 cup of Water

Directions:

1. Pour the water in your Instant Pot and place the chicken wings inside.
2. Close the lid and cook on HIGH for about 5 minutes.
3. Do a quick pressure release.
4. Rinse the wings and pat them dry with some paper towels.

5. Discard the cooking liquid and place the wings in the IP.
6. Pour the barbecue sauce over and coat them well.
7. Set the IP to SAUTE and cook until sticky on all sides.
8. Serve and enjoy!

(Calories 270| Total Fats 8g | Net Carbs: 3.6g | Protein 35g)

Spinach Duck Breast

(Total Time: 40 MIN| Serves: 6)

Ingredients:

- 2 pounds Duck Breasts, skinless and boneless
- 1 cup chopped Spinach, packed
- ½ cup Chicken Stock
- 1 tsp Oregano
- ¾ cup Heavy Cream
- 1 tsp minced Garlic
- ¼ tsp Onion Powder
- ½ cup chopped Sun-Dried Tomatoes
- ½ cup grated Parmesan Cheese

Directions:

1. Combine the garlic, onion powder, oil, and oregano, and rub the mixture into the meat.

2. Set your IP to SAUTE and cook the duck until golden on all sides.
3. Pour the stock over, close the lid, and cook on High for 5 minutes.
4. Press CANCEL and release the pressure quickly.
5. Stir in the spinach, tomatoes, and heavy cream.
6. Close the lid and cook on HIGH for another 5 minutes.
7. Do a quick pressure release again. Serve and enjoy!

(Calories 455| Total Fats 26g | Net Carbs: 1g | Protein 45g)

Thai Turkey with Basil

(Total Time: 40 MIN| Serves: 4)

Ingredients:

- 2 cups cubed Turkey Breasts
- ¼ cup chopped Basil
- 2 tbsp Avocado Oil
- 2 tsp minced Garlic
- 2 tbsp Fish Sauce
- 1 tsp minced Ginger
- 1 tsp Sweetener
- 2 tsp minced Chilies
- ¼ tsp Salt
- Pinch of White Pepper

- 1 ½ cups Water

Directions:

1. Heat 1 tbsp of oil in your Instant Pot on SAUTE.
2. Add the turkey and cook until no longer pink.
3. Transfer the turkey to a greased baking dish.
4. In a bowl, whisk together the fish sauce, garlic, ginger, chilies, sweetener, and the rest of the oil.
5. Pour this mixture over the turkey and coat with your hands to coat well.
6. Pour the water in the IP and lower the trivet.
7. Place the baking dish inside and close the lid.
8. Cook on POULTRY for 12 minutes.
9. Release the pressure quickly.
10. Serve and enjoy!

(Calories 192| Total Fats 11g| Net Carbs: 1.2g | Protein 25g)

Simple and Soft Chicken Breasts

(Total Time: 35 MIN| Serves: 6)

Ingredients:

- 4 Chicken Breasts, frozen
- 1 cup Chicken Stock
- ¼ tsp Pepper
- ¼ tsp salt
- 1 cup Water

Directions:

1. Place all of the ingredients in your Instant Pot and close the lid.
2. Set it to MANUAL.
3. Cook on HIGH for 25 minutes.
NO→4. Release the pressure quickly. N P R
5. Serve the chicken as desired and enjoy!

(Calories 270| Total Fats 11g | Net Carbs: 2g | Protein 24g)

Chicken Salad with Spinach and Sour Cream

(Total Time: 35 MIN| Serves: 6)

Ingredients:

- 1 cup Sour Cream
- 1 pound Chicken Breasts
- 3 Tomatoes, chopped
- 3 cups Baby Spinach

- 1 Avocado, sliced
- 1 tsp Garlic Powder
- Salt and Pepper, to taste
- 1 cup Water

Directions:

1. Pour the water in your Instant Pot and place the chicken in it.
2. Close and lock the lid and set the IP to MANUAL.
3. Cook on high for 20 minutes.
4. Release the pressure quickly and transfer the chicken to a cutting board.
5. Cut into slices.
6. Discard the water and place the sour cream, garlic powder and some salt and pepper, in the IP.
7. Whisk to combine.
8. Cook on SAUTE for 1 minute.
9. Combine the spinach, tomatoes, and avocado, in a large bowl.
10. Top with the sliced chicken.
11. Drizzled the sour cream over.
12. Serve and enjoy!

(Calories 360| Total Fats 32g | Net Carbs: 2.5g | Protein 27g)

Marinara Chicken

(Total Time: 25 MIN| Serves: 6)

Ingredients:

- 1 ½ pounds Chicken Meat, cut into cubes
- 15 ounces Keto Marinara sauce
- 15 ounces Chicken Broth
- 8 ounces shredded Monterrey Jack Cheese
- Salt and Pepper, to taste
- 1 tbsp chopped Parsley

Directions:

1. Place everything, except the parsley, in your Instant Pot.
2. Close and lock the lid and set it to MANUAL.
3. Cook on HIGH for 15 minutes.
4. Do a quick pressure release.
5. Transfer to a bowl and top with chopped parsley.
6. Serve and enjoy!

(Calories 270| Total Fats 17g | Net Carbs: 2g | Protein 22g)

Alfredo Chicken Keto Pasta

(Total Time: 10 MIN| Serves: 3)

Ingredients:

- 3 cups Spiralized Veggies
- 3 tbsp grated Parmesan Cheese
- 15 ounces Keto Alfredo Sauce
- ½ tsp Oregano
- ½ tsp Basil
- 1 cup cooked and shredded Chicken Meat
- Salt and Pepper, to taste

Directions:

1. Place everything but the Parmesan, in your Instant Pot.
2. Lock the lid and set it to MANUAL.
3. Cook on HIGH for 10 minutes.
4. Release the pressure quickly.
5. Serve the pasta topped with grated Parmesan cheese.
6. Enjoy!

(Calories 192| Total Fats 10.5g | Net Carbs: 3g | Protein 14g)

Sticky Chicken

(Total Time: 30 MIN| Serves: 6)

Ingredients:

- 6 Chicken Drumsticks
- 1 tbsp Olive Oil
- ½ cup sugar-free Barbecue Sauce
- ½ cup plus 2 tbsp Water
- 1 ½ tbsp Arrowroot
- 1 tsp minced Garlic
- 1 Onion, chopped

Directions:

1. Heat the oil in the Instant Pot on SAUTE and cook the onions for about 3 minutes, or until soft.
2. Add garlic and cook for 30 seconds more.
3. Add ½ cup water and the barbecue sauce and stir to combine.
4. Place the chicken drumsticks inside and close the lid.
5. Cook on MANUAL for 10 minutes.

6. Release the pressure quickly.
7. Whisk together the remaining water and arrowroot and stir into the sauce.
8. Cook n SAUTE for a few minutes, until thickened.
9. Serve the drumsticks with the sauce on the side,
10. Serve and enjoy!

(Calories 435| Total Fats 12g| Net Carbs: 7g | Protein 26.5g)

<u>Red Meat Recipes</u>

Instant Fall-Apart Beef Roast

(Total Time: 80 MIN| Serves: 4)

Ingredients:

- 1 Onion, sliced
- 2 pounds Beef Roast
- 2 cups Beef Broth
- 2 tbsp Coconut Oil
- Salt and Pepper, to taste

Directions:

1. Melt the coconut oil in your Instant Pot on SAUTE.
2. Meanwhile, season the beef with some salt and pepper.
3. Place the meat inside the IP and sear on all sides until browned.
4. Place the onion slices on top and pour the beef broth over.

5. Close the lid and cook on MANUAL for 70 minutes.
6. Do a quick pressure release.
7. Serve and enjoy!

(Calories 750| Total Fats 50g | Net Carbs: 2.5g | Protein 60g)

Rump Steak with Mushrooms in Red Wine

(Total Time: 30 MIN| Serves: 15)

Ingredients:

- 9 pounds Rump Steak
- 1 ½ cups Red Wine
- 3 tbsp Olive Oil
- 2 cups diced Celery
- 2 cups sliced Mushrooms
- 18 ounces canned Tomato Paste
- 3 Onions, chopped
- 3 Bay Leaves
- 1 tsp Salt
- 10 ounces Beef Broth

Directions:

1. Heat the olive oil in your Instant Pot on SAUTE.
2. Add the meat and sear on all sides until browned.

3. Place the veggies inside.
4. Whisk together the wine, broth, and tomato paste.
5. Pour over the meat and add the bay leaves.
6. Close the lid and cook on HIGH for 35 minutes.
7. Serve and enjoy!

(Calories 600| Total Fats 35g | Net Carbs: 7g | Protein 50g)

Worcestershire Pork Chops

(Total Time: 35 MIN| Serves: 6)

Ingredients:

- 1 Onion, diced
- 3 tbsp Worcestershire Sauce
- ¼ cup Butter
- 6 Pork Chops
- 1 cup Water
- Salt and Pepper, to taste

Directions:

1. Melt half of the butter in the IP on SAUTE.
2. Add the pork chops and cook until browned on all sides. Transfer to a plate.
3. Melt the remaining butter in the IP.
4. Add the onions and cook for 3 minutes.
5. Add the Worcestershire sauce and water.

6. Return the pork chops to the Instant Pot.
7. Close the lid and cook for 15 minutes on HIGH.
8. Do a natural pressure release/
9. Serve and enjoy!

(Calories 520| Total Fats 42g | Net Carbs: 5 g | Protein 60g)

Port and Garlic Lamb

(Total Time: 30 MIN| Serves: 4)

Ingredients:

- 1 tbsp Olive Oil
- 2 pounds Lamb Shanks
- 1 tbsp Tomato Paste
- 10 Whole Garlic Cloves
- 1 tsp Balsamic Vinegar
- ½ cup Port Wine
- 1 tsp Rosemary
- 1 tbsp Butter
- ½ cup Chicken Broth

Directions:

1. Heat the oil in your Instant Pot on SAUTE.
2. Place the lamb shanks in the pot and cook until browned on all sides.
3. Add the remaining ingredients, except for the vinegar and butter.

4. Close the lid and set to MANUAL.
5. Cook on HIGH for about 20 minutes.
6. Let the pressure come down naturally.
7. Stir in the butter and vinegar just before serving.
8. Enjoy!

(Calories 610| Total Fats 35g | Net Carbs: 8.2g | Protein 55g)

Herbed Meatloaf

(Total Time: 55 MIN| Serves: 6)

Ingredients:

- 2 pounds Ground Beef
- 1 tsp Rosemary
- 1 tsp Thyme
- 1 tsp Oregano
- 2 Eggs
- ½ tsp Garlic Powder
- 3 tbsp Olive Oil
- 1 ½ cups Water

Directions:

1. Pour the water into your Instant Pot and grease a loaf pan with the olive oil.
2. Place all of the remaining ingredients in a bowl and combine with your hands.
3. Press the mixture into the greased loaf pan (you can do it in batches if you have small loaf pans).
4. Lower the trivet and place the loaf pan inside the IP.
5. Close the lid and choose MANUAL.
6. Cook on HIGH for half an hour.
7. Do a quick pressure release.
8. Serve and enjoy!

(Calories 260| Total Fats 14g | Net Carbs: 2g | Protein 9g)

Chili Meatballs

(Total Time: 35 MIN| Serves: 4)

Ingredients:

- 1 Egg
- 1 pound Ground Beef
- ¼ cup Arrowroot
- ½ cup Chili Sauce
- 1 tbsp Worcestershire Sauce
- 1 tbsp Tamari Sauce
- ½ tsp Paprika
- ½ tsp Chili Powder
- ½ tsp Garlic Salt

Directions:

1. In a bowl, place the meat, arrowroot, salt, and egg.
2. Mix the mixture with your hands and shape into meatballs.
3. Place the remaining ingredients in your Instant Pot and whisk to combine.
4. Drop the meatballs in the sauce and close the lid.
5. Set the IP to MANUAL.
6. Cook on LOW for 30 minutes.
7. Do a quick pressure release.
8. Serve and enjoy!

(Calories 380| Total Fats 19g | Net Carbs: 5.5g | Protein 40g)

Gingery Beef with Broccoli

(Total Time: 50 MIN| Serves: 4)

Ingredients:

- 1 pound Beef, chopped
- 1 tsp minced Garlic
- 1 ½ tsp grated Ginger
- 1 Onion, quartered
- ¼ cup Coconut Aminos
- 12 ounces Broccoli Florets, frozen
- 2 tbsp Fish Sauce
- Salt and Pepper, to taste

Directions:

1. Place everything but the broccoli, in your Instant Pot.
2. Stir until combined and close the lid.
3. Cook on MEAT/STEW at the default set time.
4. When the timer goes off, release the pressure quickly.
5. Stir in the broccoli.
6. Cook on SAUTE with the lid off for 5 minutes.
7. Serve immediately.
8. Enjoy!

(Calories 270| Total Fats 12g | Net Carbs: 7 g | Protein 25)

Mediterranean Ground Beef Dish

(Total Time: 30 MIN| Serves: 4)

Ingredients:

- 1 pound ground Beef
- 8 ounces sliced Mozzarella Cheese
- 28 ounces canned Tomatoes
- 1 Spring Onion, sliced
- 1 Carrot, sliced
- 1 tbsp chopped Basil
- ½ Red Onion, drained
- 1 tbsp Red Wine
- 1 tsp Italian Seasoning
- 1 tbsp Olive Oil

Directions:

1. Heat the olive oil in your Instant Pot on SAUTE.
2. Add onion and cook for 2 minutes.
3. Add the beef and cook for a few more minutes, or until browned.

4. Stir in the remaining ingredients, except the mozzarella.
5. Close the lid and set to MANUAL.
6. Cook on HIGH for 15 minutes.
7. Do a quick pressure release.
8. Stir in the mozzarella.
9. Serve and enjoy!

(Calories 386| Total Fats 15g | Net Carbs: 7g | Protein 22g)

Creamy Mushroom Pork Chops

(Total Time: 35 MIN| Serves: 4)

Ingredients:

- 1 can of Cream of Mushroom Soup
- 2 tbsp Olive Oil
- 4 Pork Chops
- ¼ tsp Pepper
- 1 ½ cups Water

Directions:

1. Heat the oil in your Instant Pot on SAUTE.
2. Sason the pork chops with some pepper and cook them until browned on all sides. Transfer to a plate.

3. Whisk together the water and cream of mushroom soup in the pot.
4. Return the pork chops and close the lid.
5. Cook on HIGH for 18 minutes.
6. Let the pressure drop naturally, about 10 minutes.
7. Serve and enjoy!

(Calories 380| Total Fats 30g | Net Carbs: 1g | Protein 20g)

Smokey Chuck

(Total Time: 75 MIN| Serves: 8)

Ingredients:

- 2 ½ pounds Chuck Roast
- 1 tsp Thyme
- 1 tsp Garlic Powder
- 1 tsp Onion Powder
- 1 ½ tsp Cumin

- 2 tsp Liquid Smoke
- 1 tsp Sweetener
- ½ tsp Smoked Paprika
- 1 tsp Pepper
- 1 cup Beef Broth
- 1 tbsp Ghee

Directions:

1. Melt the ghee in the Instant Pot on SAUTE.
2. Season the meat with all of the spices.
3. Sear the chuck on all sides until browned.
4. Pour over the beef h and drizzle the liquid smoke/
5. Close the lid. Cook for 60 minutes on MANUAL.
6. Let the pressure release naturally.
7. Serve and enjoy!

(Calories 380| Total Fats 24g | Net Carbs: 0.9g | Protein 40g)

Flavorful Pork Butt

(Total Time: 75 MIN| Serves: 6)

Ingredients:

- 1 tbsp Olive Oil
- 2 tsp Pepper
- 4 pounds Pork Butt
- 2 tsp Oregano
- 1 tsp Cayenne Pepper
- 2 tsp Sweetener
- 2 tsp Cumin
- 1 tsp Garlic Powder
- 1 tsp Onion Powder

Directions:

1. Brush the olive oil over the meat.
2. Combine the spices in a small bowl and rub the mixture into the meat.
3. Pour enough water to cover the bottom of the IP well.
4. Place the meat inside.
5. Close the lid and cook on MANUAL for 65 minutes.
6. Wait 5 minutes before releasing the pressure quickly.
7. Serve and enjoy!

(Calories 748| Total Fats 60g | Net Carbs: 1g | Protein 55g)

Braised Lamb Shanks

(Total Time: 50 MIN| Serves: 4)

Ingredients:

- 4 Lamb Shanks
- 3 tbsp Almond Flour
- ½ Yellow Bell Pepper, diced
- 8 ounces canned diced Tomatoes
- ½ Onion, diced
- 2 tbsp Olive Oil
- 1 tsp minced Garlic
- 2/3 cup Beef Broth

Directions:

1. Place the lambs and flour in a plastic bag and shake to coat well.
2. Heat half of the oil in your IP on SAUTE.
3. Add the lamb and cook until browned on all sides. Transfer to a plate.
4. Heat the remaining oil and cook the onions and pepper for 3 minutes.

5. Add garlic and cook for another minute.
6. Stir in the tomatoes and cook for 3 more minutes,
7. Pour the broth over and stir to combine.
8. Return the shanks to the pot.
9. Close the lid and cook on HIGH for 25 minutes.
10. Let the pressure drop naturally.
11. Serve the lamb drizzled with some of the cooking sauce.
12. Serve and enjoy!

(Calories 590| Total Fats 40g | Net Carbs: 7.2g | Protein 53g)

Sweet and Sticky Short Ribs

(Total Time: 4 hours and 40 MIN| Serves: 4)

Ingredients:

- 2 tbsp Sweetener
- ¾ cup Soy Sauce
- 4 Beef Short Ribs

- 1 Garlic Head, crushed Juice of 1 Orange
- ½ tbsp Sesame Oil
- 1 tsp minced Ginger
- 1 cup of Water
- 2 tsp Arrowroot

Directions:

1. Place everything, except the arrowroot,in a bowl.
2. Stir to combine well.
3. Cover the bowl and place in the fridge to marinate for 4 hours.
4. Transfer everything to the Instant Pot.
5. Close the lid and cook for 30 minutes on HIGH.
6. Release the pressure naturally and transfer the ribs to a plate.o
7. Whisk the arrowroot and let cook on SAUTE until thickened.
8. Transfer the sauce to a small bowl and serve alongside the ribs.
9. Serve and enjoy!

(Calories 490| Total Fats 12g | Net Carbs: 8g | Protein 35g)

Seafood Recipes

Seafood Paella

(Total Time: 17 MIN| Serves: 4)

Ingredients:

- 2 cups Mussels
- 2 cups ground Cauliflower
- 2 cups Fish Stock
- 1 cup Scallops
- 2 Bell Peppers, diced
- 1 tbsp Coconut Oil
- Pinch of Saffron
- ½ Onion, diced

Directions:

1. Melt the coconut oil in the Instant Pot.
2. Add onion and peppers and cook for 3-4 minutes.
3. Add the saffron and scallops and continue cooking for 2 more minutes.
4. Stir in the fish stock, mussels, and cauliflower.

5. Close the lid and choose MANUAL.
6. Cook on HIGH for 6 minutes.
7. Do a quick pressure release.
8. Serve and enjoy!

(Calories 155| Total Fats 5g | Net Carbs: 6.8g | Protein 7g)

Festive Oysters

(Total Time: 15 MIN| Serves: 6)

Ingredients:

- 6 tbsp Butter, melted
- 36 Oysters
- 1 cup Water

Directions:

1. Clean the oysters thoroughly and place in the Instant Pot.
2. Pour the water over and close the lid.

3. Cook on HIGH for 3 minutes.
4. Let the pressure release naturally.
5. Serve the oysters drizzled with butter.
6. Enjoy!

(Calories 142| Total Fats 12.3g | Net Carbs: 1g | Protein 7g)

Tomato Prawns

(Total Time: 10 MIN| Serves: 4)

Ingredients:

- 1 pound Prawns
- 1 cup canned diced Tomatoes
- ½ cup Tomato Sauce
- 1 tsp Garlic Powder
- ½ tsp Onion Powder
- ¼ tsp Pepper
- 2 Spring Onions - green parts only, chopped

Directions:

1. Place all of the ingredients in the Instant Pot.
2. Stir to combine well.
3. Close and lock the lid and choose MANUAL.
4. Cook on HIGH for 4 minutes.
5. Release the pressure quickly.
6. Serve and enjoy!

(Calories 149| Total Fats 9g | Net Carbs: 3.6g | Protein 11g)

Clams in White Wine

(Total Time: 17 MIN| Serves: 4)

Ingredients:

- 2 cups Vegetable Broth
- ¼ cup White Wine
- 2 tbsp Lemon Juice
- 2 tsp minced Garlic
- 2 ½ pounds Clams
- ¼ cup chopped Basil
- ¼ cup Olive Oil

Directions:

1. Heat the oil in your Instant Pot on SAUTE.
2. Add the garlic and cook for a minute, or just until fragrant.
3. Add the wine, broth, lemon juice, and basil.

4. When the mixture starts to boil, place the clams in the steaming basket and lower it.
5. Close the lid and cook on HIGH for 4 minutes.
6. Serve and enjoy!

(Calories 225| Total Fats 15g | Net Carbs: 5.5g | Protein 16g)

Almond Tilapia

(Total Time: 10 MIN| Serves: 4)

Ingredients:

- 4 Tilapia Fillets
- 1 tsp Olive Oil
- 2 tbsp Dijon Mustard
- 2/3 cup sliced Almonds
- ¼ tsp Lemon Pepper
- 1 cup Water

Directions:

1. Pour the water into your Instant Pot and lower the rack.
2. Whisk together the oil, mustard, and pepper.
3. Brush the almond fillets with the mixture.
4. Coat the tilapia in sliced almonds.
5. Arrange on the rack of the Instant Pot.
6. Close the lid and cook for 5 minutes on HIGH.
7. Do a quick pressure release.

8. Serve and enjoy!

(Calories 326| Total Fats 15g | Net Carbs: 1.3g | Protein 44g)

Lemon Pepper Salmon

(Total Time: 10 MIN| Serves: 4)

Ingredients:

- 4 Salmon Fillets
- 1 ½ cups Water
- 1 tsp Lemon Pepper
- Juice from 1 Lemon
- 8 Lemon Slices

Directions:

1. Pour the water into the Instant Pot. Lower the rack.
2. Season the salmon with the lemon pepper.
3. Arrange it on the rack, drizzle with lemon juice, and place lemon slices on top.

4. Close the lid and choose MANUAL.
5. Cook on HIGH for 4 minutes.
6. Serve and enjoy!

(Calories 180| Total Fats 8g | Net Carbs: 1.5g | Protein 25g)

Simple Lobster Tails

(Total Time: 25 MIN| Serves: 4)

Ingredients:

- 4 Lobster Tails
- 1 cup Water
- ½ cup White Wine
- ½ cup Butter, melted

Directions:

1. Pour the water and the white wine in the Instant Pot. Lower the steaming basket.
2. Cut the lobster tails in half and place them in the basket.
3. Close the lid and choose MANUAL.
4. Cook on LOW for 5 minutes.
5. Do a natural pressure release.
6. Place on a platter and drizzle with melted butter.
7. Serve and enjoy!

(Calories 190| Total Fats 12g | Net Carbs: 0g | Protein 19g)

Cheddar Haddock

(Total Time: 35 MIN| Serves: 4)

Ingredients:

- ½ cup Heavy Cream
- 12 ounces Haddock
- 5 ounces Cheddar Cheese, gratd
- 1 tbsp Butter
- 1 tsp ground Ginger
- ¼ tsp Pepper
- ¼ tsp Salt

Directions:

1. Season the haddock with the ginger, garlic, pepper, and salt.
2. Melt the butter in the Instant Pot on SAUTE.
3. Add the haddock and cook on SAUTE for about 2 minutes per side.
4. Pour the cream over and top with the cheese.
5. Close the lid and cook on HIGH for 2 minutes.
6. Do a quick pressure release.
7. Serve and enjoy!

(Calories 195| Total Fats 18g | Net Carbs: 6.5g | Protein 18g)

Lime and Garlic Octopus

(Total Time: 20 MIN| Serves: 4)

Ingredients:

- 10 ounces Octopus
- 1 tsp chopped Cilantro
- 2 tbsp Olive Oil
- 2 tsp Garlic Powder
- 3 tbsp Lime Juice
- Salt and Pepper, to taste
- 1 ½ cups Water

Directions:

1. Pour the water into the Instant Pot.
2. Stir in the garlic, salt, pepper, and cilantro.
3. Add the octopus and close the lid.
4. Choose MANUAL and cook on HIGH for 8 minutes.
5. Do a quick pressure release.
6. Drizzle with lime juice.
7. Serve and enjoy!

(Calories 120| Total Fats 3g | Net Carbs: 2.5g | Protein 9g)

Shrimp on Asparagus

(Total Time: 25 MIN| Serves: 4)

Ingredients:

- 1 tbsp Cajun Seasoning
- 1 Asparagus Bunch, trimmed
- 1 pound Shrimp, peeled and deveined
- 1 tsp Olive Oil
- 1 ½ cups Water

Directions:

1. Pour the water into the Instant Pot. Lower the rack.
2. Arrange the asparagus on the rack, but in a single layer.
3. Place the shrimp on top, again, in a single layer.
4. Drizzle with oil and sprinkle with Cajun seasoning.
5. Close the lid and choose STEAM.
6. Cook for 2 minutes.
7. Do a quick pressure release.
8. Serve and enjoy!

(Calories 320| Total Fats 10g | Net Carbs: 9g | Protein 40g)

Buttery and Garlicky Crab Legs

(Total Time: 10 MIN| Serves: 4)

Ingredients:

- 1/3 cup Butter
- 2 tsp minced Garlic
- 3 pounds Crab Legs
- 1 tsp Olive Oil
- 1 ½ cups Water

Directions:

1. Pour the water into the Instant Pot.
2. Place the crab legs in the steaming basket and lower it.
3. Close the lid and choose STEAM.
4. Cook for 3 minutes.
5. Transfer the crab legs to a serving plate.
6. Discard the water and melt the butter with the olive oil, in the Instant Pot.
7. Add garlic and cook for 1 minute.
8. Drizzle the garlicky butter over the crab legs.
9. Serve and enjoy!

(Calories 300| Total Fats 6g | Net Carbs: 3g | Protein 35g)

Mediterranean Salmon

(Total Time: 15 MIN| Serves: 4)

Ingredients:

- 1 cup Cherry Tomatoes
- 15 ounces Asparagus
- 1 cup Baby Carrots
- 1 Rosemary Sprig
- 4 Frozen Salmon Fillets
- 1 cup Water

Directions:

1. Pour the water into the Instant Pot. Lower the rack.
2. Arrange the salmon on the place the rosemary on top.
3. Top with the asparagus spears. Arrange the carrots on the side.
4. Close the lid and cook on HIGH for 90 seconds.
5. Release the pressure quickly.
6. Top with cherry tomatoes and close the lid again.
7. Cook for 2 more minutes.
8. Do a quick pressure release again.
9. Serve and enjoy!

(Calories 470| Total Fats 31g | Net Carbs: 6.3g | Protein 42g)

<u>Vegetarian Recipes</u>

Fake Wild Mushroom Risotto

(Total Time: 10 MIN| Serves: 4)

Ingredients:

- 1 Large Cauliflower Head, riced
- 1 cups Veggie Broth
- ½ Onion, diced
- 2 cups Wild Mushrooms Slices
- 4 tbsp grated Parmesan Cheese
- 1 tbsp Butter
- ½ tsp Thyme
- ¼ tsp Oregano
- 1 tsp minced Garlic

Directions:

1. Heat the oil in the Instant Pot.
2. Add the onions and cook for 3 minutes.
3. Add garlic and cook for 30 more seconds.
4. Stir in the mushroom slices and cook for 3-5 minutes.
5. Add the remaining ingredients, except the cheese.
6. Give the mixture a stir so you can combine everything well.
7. Close the lid and cook for 5 minutes on HIGH.
8. Do a quick pressure release.
9. Serve topped with the Parmesan cheese.

(Calories 110| Total Fats 12g | Net Carbs: 6g | Protein 2.5g)

A Different Ratatouille

(Total Time: 20 MIN| Serves: 4)

Ingredients:

- 1 ½ Large Zucchini
- 1 ½ Large Eggplant
- 3 Large Tomatoes, sliced
- 1 tsp mince Garlic
- 1 tbsp Olive Oil
- Salt and Pepper, to taste
- 1 ½ cups Water

Directions:

1. Pour the water in your Instant Pot and lower the trivet.
2. Grease a round baking dish with cooking spray.
3. Arrange a layer of zucchini slices to cover the bottom of the dish. Then top with a layer of eggplant slices, and finally a layer of diced tomatoes. Repeat until you have no more ingredients left.
4. Drizzle the veggies with olive oil.

5. Sprinkle with the garlic, and some salt and pepper.
6. Place the dish in the IP and close the lid.
7. Cook on HIGH for 10 minutes.
8. Serve and enjoy!

(Calories 180| Total Fats 10g | Net Carbs: 6.5g | Protein 2.5g)

Vegetarian Burger Patties

(Total Time: 20 MIN| Serves: 3)

Ingredients:

- 1 Zucchini, chopped
- 1 cup Cauliflower Florets
- 1 cup Broccoli Florets
- ½ cup Almond Flour
- 1 Egg
- ½ tsp minced Garlic
- ½ Onion, diced
- 1 tsp Cumin
- ¼ tsp Pepper
- ¼ tsp Salt
- 1 tbsp Olive Oil
- 1 ½ cups Water

Directions:

1. Place the veggies, egg, flour, and spices, in a food processor.

2. Process until ground.
3. Make 3 patties out of the mixture.
4. Heat the oil in your Instant Pot and cook the patties until golden on all sides.
5. Transfer to a baking dish that has been previously greased.
6. Pour the water in your Instant Pot and lower the trivet.
7. Place the dish inside and close the lid.
8. Let cook for 5 minutes on HIGH.
9. Do a quick pressure release.
10. Serve and enjoy!

(Calories 148| Total Fats 4g | Net Carbs: 4.5g | Protein 4g)

Greek Keto Pasta

(Total Time: 15 MIN| Serves: 4)

Ingredients:

- 1 cup Spinach
- ¼ cup Parmesan Cheese
- 10 Kalamata Olives
- 2 tbsp Butter
- ¼ cup crumbled Feta Cheese
- 2 tbsp Capers
- 2 large Zucchini, spiralized
- 2 tsp minced Garlic
- ¼ cup chopped Sun-Dried Tomatoes
- 1 cup Veggie Broth

Directions:

1. Melt the butter in your Instant Pot and cook the garlic for one minute.
2. Add zoodles and spinach and cook for 1 minute.
3. Pour the broth over along with the remaining ingredients.
4. Close the lid and cook for 3 minutes on MANUAL.
5. Drain the pasta and serve.
6. Serve and enjoy!

(Calories 230| Total Fats 20g | Net Carbs: 6.5g | Protein 6.4g)

Keto Grilled Cheese

(Total Time: 20 MIN| Serves: 4)

Ingredients:

- 2 ounces Cheddar Cheese
- 2 tbsp Almond Flour
- 2 Eggs
- ½ tsp Baking Powder
- 1 ½ tbsp Psyllium Husk Powder
- 3 tbsp Butter

Directions:

1. Place 1 tbsp butter, flour, eggs, psyllium husk, and baking powder, in a microwave-safe dish.
2. Microwave for 90 seconds.
3. Let cool completely.
4. Cut the 'bun' in half and spread the butter on the outsides.
5. Place the cheddar on one half and top with the other.
6. Set your Instant Pot to SAUTE.
7. Coat with cooking spray and place the sandwich inside.
8. Cook for about 3 minutes per side, or until golden and crispy.
9. Serve and enjoy!

(Calories 800| Total Fats 69g | Net Carbs: 6.5g | Protein 25g)

Keto Mac and Cheese

(Total Time: 45 MIN| Serves: 4)

Ingredients:

- 1 Cauliflower Head, chopped
- 1 ½ cups shredded Cheddar Cheese
- 1 tsp Turmeric
- 3 Eggs
- 1/4 cup Cream
- 1 cup Water

Directions:

1. Pour the water in your Instant Pot and lower the trivet.
2. Place the cauliflower in the microwave and microwave for 5 minutes.
3. Grease baking dish and transfer the cauliflower to it.
4. Beat the eggs along with the cream and turmeric.
5. Pour over the cauliflower.
6. Top with the shredded cheese.
7. Place the dish inside the Instant Pot.

8. Close the lid and choose MANUAL.
9. Cook on HIGH for 10 minutes.
10. Serve and enjoy!

(Calories 280| Total Fats 21g | Net Carbs: 3.5g | Protein 15g)

Mexican Cauliflower Dish

(Total Time: 15 MIN| Serves: 4)

Ingredients:

- 2 cups Cauliflower Florets
- ½ tsp Paprika
- 1 tsp Chili Powder
- 1 cup canned diced Tomatoes
- ¼ Red Onion, minced
- 1 cup Water
- ¼ cup Nutritional Yeast
- ¼ cup chopped Nuts
- ½ cup chopped Celery

Directions:

1. Pour the water in your Instant Pot.
2. Add the cauliflower, celery,, and nuts.
3. Close the lid and cook for 5 minutes on HIGH.
4. Drain the veggies and transfer to a blender.
5. Add the chili powder, paprika, and yeast.
6. Stir in the canned tomatoes and onions.

7. Serve and enjoy!

(Calories 100| Total Fats 4| Net Carbs: 6g | Protein 5.5g)

Garlicky Zucchini and Cherry Tomato Pasta

(Total Time: 20 MIN| Serves: 4)

Ingredients:

- 6 cups spiralized Zucchini
- 2 tsp minced Garlic
- ¼ cup chopped Basil
- ½ cup Tomato Sauce
- ¼ cup Veggie Broth
- 1 tbsp Olive Oil
- 1 cup Cherry Tomatoes, halved\
- ½ cup shredded Mozzarella Cheese

Directions:

1. Place all of the ingredients in your Instant Pot.
2. Stir well to combine and close the lid.
3. Set your Instant Pot to MNUAL.
4. Cook on HIGH for 3 minutes.
5. Do a quick pressure release.
6. Stir in the mozzarella and serve.

(Calories 211| Total Fats 9g | Net Carbs: 6g | Protein 4.5g)

White Pizza

(Total Time: 15 MIN| Serves: 2)

Ingredients:

- 1 Keto Pizza Crust, store bought (made with nut flour and with allowed ingredients only)
- ¼ cup Keto Alfredo Sauce
- ½ cup shredded Mozzarella Cheese
- 1 tsp chopped Oregano
- 1 ½ cups Water

Directions:

1. Pour the water in your Instant Pot and lower the trivet.
2. Grease a round baking dish that can fit inside your Instant Pot.
3. Place the Keto pizza crust and spread the Alfredo sauce over.
4. Sprinkle with cheese.
5. Place in the Instant Pot and close the lid.
6. Cook on MANUAL for 5 minutes.
7. Do a quick pressure release.
8. Sprinkle with oregano and slice.
9. Serve and enjoy!

(Calories 390| Total Fats 20g | Net Carbs: 5.8g | Protein 8g)

Stocks and Sauces

Instant Fish Stock

(Total Time: 70 MIN| Serves: 6)

Ingredients:

- 1 cup Celery, chopped
- 2 Fish Heads, chopped
- 1 cup Carrots, chopped
- 1 tbsp Olive Oil
- 2 Lemongrass Stalks, chopped
- 2 tsp minced Garlic
- 1 tbsp minced Onion
- 1 tbsp Thyme

Directions:

1. Set your Instant Pot to SAUTE.
2. Heat the olive oil in it and add the fish heads.
3. Cook for 2 minutes.
4. Add carrots, celery, onion, garlic, and thyme.
5. Cook for 2 more minutes.
6. Pour over about 3 quarts of water.
7. Close the lid and cook on HIGH for 45 minutes.
8. Let the pressure release naturally, for about 15-20 minutes. Strain the broth and store/

(Calories 45| Total Fats 2g | Net Carbs: 0g | Protein 6g)

Bone Broth

(Total Time: 110 MIN| Serves: 4)

Ingredients:

- 1 ½ pounds Bones, this recipes uses Beef
- 2 tsp minced Garlic
- 2 Thyme Sprigs
- 1 Onion, chopped
- 1/3 cup chopped Celery
- ½ cup chopped Carrots
- 3 Bay Leaves
- 1 tsp Salt

Directions:

1. Place everything in the Instant Pot and stir to combine.
2. Pour water over, but make sure it doesn't go over the max line.
3. Lock the lid and choose MANUAL.
4. Cook on HIGH for 90 minutes.
5. Let the pressure drop naturally.
6. Strain the broth and store.

(Calories 25| Total Fats 1g | Net Carbs: 0g | Protein 3g)

Simple Chicken Stock

(Total Time: 140 MIN| Serves: 4)

Ingredients:

- 1 Chicken Carcass
- A handful of Peppercorns
- 1 Onion, chopped
- 1 tbsp Apple Cider Vinegar
- 1 Carrot, quartered
- ½ cup Celery Root, chopped
- 1 tsp Salt

Directions:

1. Place all of the ingredients in the Instant Pot.
2. Add water to cover everything well. Make sure it doesn't go above the max line.
3. Close the lid and choose the SOUP cooking mode.
4. Cook for 120 minutes.
5. Release the pressure for 15 minutes.
6. Strain the broth and store.

(Calories 50| Total Fats 3g | Net Carbs: 1g | Protein 10g)

Pomodoro Basil Sauce

(Total Time: 40 MIN| Serves: 4)

Ingredients:

- 1 tbsp Olive Oil
- 2 tsp minced Garlic
- ½ Onion, diced
- 2 ½ pounds Tomatoes, diced
- ½ cup chopped Basil
- 1 tbsp Italian Seasoning
- ¼ tsp Pepper
- ¼ tsp Sweetener
- 1 tsp Salt

Directions:

1. Heat the olive oil in your Instant Pot on SAUTE.
2. Add the onions and cook for 2 minutes.
3. Add garlic and cook for one more minute.
4. Place the rest of the ingredients inside and stir to combine.
5. Lock the lid and choose MANUAL.
6. Cook for 12 minutes on HIGH.
7. Do a quick pressure release.
8. Set it to SAUTE and cook for another 5 minutes.
9. Serve immediately or let cool and store.

(Calories 40| Total Fats 2g | Net Carbs: 4g | Protein 1.2g)

Homemade Salsa

(Total Time: 25 MIN| Serves: 6)

Ingredients:

- 6 ounces Hot Peppers, without the stems
- 2 cups diced Tomatoes, canned
- ½ cup Apple Cider Vinegar
- 1 tsp Salt
- ¼ tsp Sweetener
- ¼ tsp Garlic Powder

Directions:

1. Set your IP to SAUTE.
2. Place the tomatoes and peppers with some of the vinegar and cook for 5 minutes.
3. Stir in the remaining ingredients and close the lid.
4. Cook on MANUAL for 3 minutes.
5. Let the pressure drop naturally.
6. Transfer to a blender and blend until smooth.
7. Serve and enjoy!

(Calories 2| Total Fats 1.3g | Net Carbs: 2.2g | Protein1)

Instant Bolognese Sauce

(Total Time: 15 MIN| Serves: 4)

Ingredients:

- 1 pound Ground Beef
- 2 tsp minced Garlic
- ¼ cup chopped Parsley
- 1 tsp Basil
- 1 can Pasta Sauce, low-carb
- ¼ tsp Sweetener
- ¼ tsp Pepper

Directions:

1. Place everything in the Instant Pot.
2. Stir to combine and lock the lid.
3. Choose MANUAL and cook on HIGH for 8 minutes.
4. Do a quick pressure release.
5. Serve immediately or store.
6. Enjoy!

(Calories 360| Total Fats 12g | Net Carbs: 5g | Protein 35g)

Keto and Vegan Alfredo

(Total Time: 20 MIN| Serves: 4)

Ingredients:

- 12 ounces Cauliflower Florets
- 2 tbsp Almond Milk
- ½ cup Water
- ¼ tsp Salt
- ¼ tsp Pepper
- ¼ tsp Garlic Powder
- Pinch of Onion Powder
- Pinch of Nutmeg

Directions:

1. Place everything but the milk, in the Instant Pot.
2. Close the lid and choose MANUAL.
3. Cook on HIGH for 3 minutes.
4. Press CANCEL and do a quick pressure release.
5. Transfer the mixture to a blender.
6. Blend until smooth.
7. Stir in the milk
8. Serve and enjoy!

(Calories 40| Total Fats 0g | Net Carbs: 4g | Protein 3g)

Dessert Recipes

Apple Tart

(Total Time: 45 MIN| Serves: 8)

Ingredients:

- 1 tsp Cinnamon
- 6 tbsp Butter
- 2 cups Almond Flour
- ¼ tsp Lemon Zest
- 1/3 cup Sweetener

Filling:

- ½ tsp Cinnamon
- ¼ tsp Lemon Zest
- 3 cups sliced Apples
- ¼ cup Butter
- ¼ cup Sweetener

Topping:

- ¼ tsp Cinnamon
- 1 tbsp Sweetener

Directions:

1. Place all of the crust ingredients in a bowl.
2. Mix with your hands to combine.
3. Grease a baking dish that can fit in yout IP, with cooking spray.
4. Press the crust into it.
5. Pour 1 ½ cups of water into your Instant Pot and place the dish inside.
6. Close and cook on HIGH for 3 minutes.
7. Meanwhile, combine the lemon juice and apples and let sit.
8. Arrange the apple slices over the cooked crust.
9. Whisk the other filling ingredients. Pour the mixture over the apples.
10. Return the dish to the Instant Pot and close the lid.
11. Cook on MANUAL for 30 minutes.
12. Do a quick pressure release.
13. Combine the sweetener and cinnamon and sprinkle over the tart.
14. Serve and enjoy!

(Calories 300| Total Fats 25g | Net Carbs: 7.5g | Protein 7g)

Pecan Cookies

(Total Time: 30 MIN| Serves: 12)

Ingredients:

- 1 Egg
- 20 Pecan Halves
- 2 cups ground Pecans
- 1 tbsp Butter
- ¼ cup Sweetener
- ½ tsp Baking Soda
- 1 ½ cups Water

Directions:

1. Pour the water in your Instant Pot and lower the trivet.
2. Combine everything but the pecan halves in a bowl. Mix to combine.
3. Make 20 balls out of the mixture.
4. Line a baking dish with parchment paper.
5. Arrange 10 balls on it and place a pecan half on top.
6. Press the pecans to flatten the cookies.
7. Place the dish in the IP and close the lid.
8. Cook on HIGH for 8 minutes.
9. Repeat with the remaining cookies.
10. Serve and enjoy!

(Calories 100| Total Fats 11g | Net Carbs: 1g | Protein 1.5g)

Almond and Chocolate Cake

(Total Time: 40 MIN| Serves: 15)

Ingredients:

- 2 ½ cups Almond Flour
- 6 ounces Yogurt
- 4 Eggs
- 2 tsp Baking Powder
- 6 tbsp Milk
- ¼ cup Vanilla Whey Protein Powder
- 1 tsp Xanthan Gum
- 6 tbsp Butter
- 1 tbsp Sweetener
- ¼ cup chopped Almonds
- ½ cup Dark Chocolate, chopped
- ½ cup Oat Fiber
- Pinch of Salt

Directions:

1. Pour the water in your Instant Pot. Lower the trivet.
2. Whisk the wet ingredients in one bowl.
3. Place the dry ones in another and mix to combine.
4. Combine the two mixtures.
5. Fold in the almonds and chocolate.
6. Grease a baking pan (a loaf pan or a bundt pan) with cooking spray.

7. Pour the batter into it.
8. Place the pan in the IP and close the lid.
9. Cook on HIGH for 30 minutes.
10. Do a quick pressure release.
11. Serve and enjoy!

(Calories 180| Total Fats 12g | Net Carbs: 3g | Protein 11.7g)

Raspberry Cobbler-Like Cake

(Total Time: 40 MIN| Serves: 4)

Ingredients:

- 1 cup Raspberries
- 2 tbsp Heavy Cream
- 2 tsp Lemon Juice
- 10 Stevia drops
- 5 Egg Yolks
- ½ tsp Lemon Zest
- ¼ tsp Baking Powder
- 2 tbsp Coconut Oil

- ¼ cup Coconut Flour
- 2 tbsp Erythritol
- 1 ½ cups Water

Directions:

1. Pour the water in your IP and lower the trivet.
2. In a bowl, combine the wet ingredients.
3. In another, whisk together the dry ones.
4. Gently combine the mixtures.
5. Whisk until smooth.
6. Grease a baking dish with cooking spray.
7. Pour half of the batter into the dish.
8. Arrange the raspberries on top.
9. Top with the remaining batter.
10. Place the dish in the Instant Pot and close the lid.
11. Cook on HIGH for 15-20 minutes.
12. Serve and enjoy!

(Calories 460| Total Fats 45g | Net Carbs: 5g | Protein 9g)

Poppy Seed and Lemon Muffins

(Total Time: 25 MIN| Serves: 4)

Ingredients:

- 1 cup Coconut Flour
- 1 tbsp Lemon Juice
- ½ tsp Lemon Zest

- 1 tbsp Swerve
- 1 Egg
- 1 tsp melted Coconut Oil
- ¼ cup Coconut Milk
- 1/8 tsp Baking Soda
- Pinch of Salt
- 1 tbsp Poppy Seeds
- 1 ½ cups Water

Directions:

1. Pour the water in your Instant Pot. Lower the rack.
2. Whisk together the juice, swerve, milk, egg, and coconut milk.
3. Add the dry ingredients and whisk until smooth.
4. Divide the batter between silicone muffin cups.
5. Place the muffins on the rack and close your Instant Pot.
6. Choose MANUAL and cook for 15 minutes.
7. Do a quick pressure release.
8. Serve and enjoy!

(Calories 120| Total Fats 6g | Net Carbs: 4g | Protein 4.5g)

Nutty Coconut Muffins

(Total Time: 40 MIN| Serves: 8)

Ingredients:

- ½ cup chopped Pecans
- 3 Eggs
- ¼ cup Coconut Oil
- 1 tsp Baking Powder
- 1/3 cup Truvia
- 1 cup Almond Flour
- 1 cup Coconut Flakes
- 1 tsp Apple Pie Spice
- ½ cup Heavy Cream
- Pinch of Sea Salt
- 1 ½ cups Water

Directions:

1. Pour the water inside your IP. Lower the rack.
2. Place all of the ingredients, except the coconut and pecans, in a bowl.
3. Mix with a mixture, until really smooth and fluffy.
4. Fold in the pecans and ¾ of the coconut.
5. Divide the mixture between 8 muffin cups and place on the rack.
6. Close the lid and choose MANUAL.

7. Cook on HIGH for 15 minutes.
8. Do a quick pressure release.
9. Sprinkle the remaining coconut over.
10. Serve and enjoy!

(Calories 266| Total Fats 23.7g | Net Carbs: 4g | Protein 6.1g)

Instant Cherry Clafoutis

(Total Time: 45 MIN| Serves: 8)

Ingredients:

- 1 cup Milk
- 6 Eggs
- 1 cup Almond Flour
- ½ tsp Cherry Extract
- 1 tbsp Butter
- 1/3 cup Swerve
- 1 tbsp Vanilla
- 1 ½ cups halved Cherries
- ½ tsp Xanthan Gum
- ¼ cup Heavy Cream
- 1/8 tsp Salt
- 1 ½ cups Water

Directions:

1. Pour the water in your Instant Pot and lower the trivet.

2. Grease a baking pan with the butter.
3. Place everything in a food processor, except the cherries.
4. Pour the batter into the dish.
5. Arrange the cherries on top with the skin side down.
6. Place the dish in the IP.
7. Close and cook on MANUAL for 30 minutes.
8. Let the pressure release for 5-10 minutes.
9. Serve and enjoy!

(Calories 195| Total Fats 15g | Net Carbs: 6g | Protein 8g)

Sweet and Soft Biscuit Cookie

(Total Time: 40 MIN| Serves: 8)

Ingredients:

- ½ cup Butter
- 1 cup Coconut Flour
- 3 tbsp Swerve
- 2 tbsp Gluten-Free Baking Mix
- 3 Eggs
- 1 ½ tsp Baking Powder
- 1 tbsp Vanilla Protein Powder
- ¼ tsp Xanthan Gum
- ¾ cup Milk
- 1 ½ cups Water

Directions:

1. Pour the water in your Instant Pot and lower the trivet.
2. Place all of the dry ingredients in a bowl. Stir to combine.
3. Whisk the wet ones in another bowl.
4. Combine the two mixtures gently.
5. Knead the dough with your hands and roll it out on a flat surface.
6. Cut into small squares.
7. Arrange on a lined baking dish and place in the IP. (You may need to work in batches).
8. Close the lid and cook for 10 minutes on HIGH.
9. Release the pressure quickly,
10. Serve and enjoy!

(Calories 200| Total Fats 17g | Net Carbs: 4g | Protein 5g)

Plantain Bread

(Total Time: 55 MIN| Serves: 12)

Ingredients:

- 4 Plantains, mashed
- 1/3 cup chopped Walnuts
- 3 tbsp Butter, melted
- 1 tsp Baking Powder
- 2 cups Almond Flour
- 2 Eggs, beaten
- 3 tbsp Sweetener
- 1 tbsp Vanilla
- 1 ½ cups Water

Directions:

1. Pour the water in your Instant Pot and lower the trivet.
2. Combine the vanilla, butter, plantains, and eggs.
3. Add the dry ingredients and whisk to combine everything until smooth.
4. Grease a loaf pan and pour the batter into it.
5. Place the pan in the IP and close the lid.
6. Cook on MANUAL for 40 minutes.
7. Do a quick pressure release.
8. Serve and enjoy!

(Calories 105| Total Fats 4g | Net Carbs: 8.5g | Protein 2g)

Plum Cake

(Total Time: 40 MIN| Serves: 8)

Ingredients:

- 1 ½ cups Almond Flour
- ¼ tsp Almond Extract
- 3 Eggs
- ½ cup Butter, softened
- ½ cup Coconut Flour
- 1 tbsp Vanilla
- ¾ cup Almond Milk
- 4 Plums, halveo
- ¼ tsp Xanthan Gum
- 2 tsp Baking Powder
- ½ cup Granulated Sweetener
- Pinch of Salt
- 1 ½ cups Water

Directions:

1. Pour the water in your Instant Pot and lower the trivet.
2. Beat the butter with the sweetener until smooth.
3. Add the eggs and beat until creamy.
4. Beat in the rest of the ingredients until smooth batter forms.
5. Grease a baking dish and pour the batter into it.
6. Top with the plums, with the cut side down.
7. Place the dish in the IP and close the lid.
8. Cook on HIGH for 25 minutes.
9. Serve and enjoy!

(Calories 300| Total Fats 25g | Net Carbs: 6.5 | Protein 9.2g)

Brownie Muffins

(Total Time: 30 MIN| Serves: 6)

Ingredients:

- 1 cup Flaxseed Meal
- ¼ cup Cocoa Powder
- 1 Egg
- 1 tsp Vanilla
- ½ cup Pumpkin Puree
- 1 tsp Apple Cider Vinegar
- 2 tbsp melted Coconut Oil
- 1 tsp Vanilla
- ¼ cup sugar-free Caramel Syrup
- 1 tbsp Swerve
- 1 ½ cups Water

Directions:

1. Pour the water in your Instant Pot and lower the trivet.
2. Whisk the wet ingredients in a bowl.

3. Gently add the dry ones while whisking constantly, to avoid any lumps.
4. Divide the brownie mixture between 6 muffin cups.
5. Arrange the muffin cups on the IP's rack and close the lid.
6. Cook for 20 minutes on MANUAL.
7. Release the pressure quickly.
8. Serve and enjoy!

(Calories 193| Total Fats 14g | Net Carbs: 4.5g | Protein 7g)

Conclusion

Now that your recipe folder is richer by 100 amazingly delightful and irresistible Instant Keto recipes, the next step is to simply pick a favorite and start cooking. And if you are one of those people that love good challenges, I dare you to try them all. Satisfied taste buds are guaranteed.

Did you find these recipes tasty? Leave a review and share your cooking experience with the other readers. Your feedback will be greatly appreciated.

Thank you and happy carbless pressure cooking!

Made in the USA
San Bernardino, CA
24 July 2018